Why Does Mummy Cry? by Karyn Ward

ISBN 978-1-952027-59-8 (Paperback)
ISBN 978-1-952027-60-4 (Hardback)
ISBN 978-1-952027-61-1 (eBook)

This book is written to provide information and motivation to readers. Its purpose is not to render any type of psychological, legal, or professional advice of any kind. The content is the sole opinion and expression of the author, and not necessarily that of the publisher.

Copyright © 2020 by Karyn Ward

All rights reserved. No part of this book may be reproduced, transmitted, or distributed in any form by any means, including, but not limited to, recording, photocopying, or taking screenshots of parts of the book, without prior written permission from the author or the publisher. Brief quotations for noncommercial purposes, such as book reviews, permitted by Fair Use of the U.S. Copyright Law, are allowed without written permissions, as long as such quotations do not cause damage to the book's commercial value. For permissions, write to the publisher, whose address is stated below.

Printed in the United States of America.

New Leaf Media, LLC
175 S. 3rd Street, Suite 200
Columbus, OH 43215
www.thenewleafmedia.com

Dedicated to my five beautiful children who have shown so much compassion.

Also to my rocks, my mum Colleen and husband Wayne.

My friends should also be included but there are too many to list, but you know who you are!

Why does my mummy cry, I don't know why.

She seems so sad all the time now,

but was so happy a long time ago.

My mummy used to take me to the park
to go play all the time.
But now she hides in her room,
so I don't hear her cry.

I heard my mummy tell her friends,

on one of our few playdates,

that she has something called a chronic illness.

I don't know what that means.

I know I should ask her but I'm scared.

Does it mean I will lose my mummy?

Once my mummy used to cook all the time,
play games and read me books.
Now she doesnt have energy
and needs so much sleep.

My noise seems to make her feel worse

so I try to be good and quiet.

Because she is sad I feel so sad.

So I asked my mummy why does she cry.

My mummy sat me down

and told me she has a chronic illness.

Mum said she has something called Trigemnal Neuralgia,

but she says there are so many other chronic illnesses.

She has friends with Multiple Sclorosis and Crohns.

Ones with fibromyalgia and depression.

Nana has Restless Legs and my friends have Diabetes.

Mum said so many other people have other conditions, and not just mummys but daddys and grandparents too.

She told me how it effects her,
like the wind and rain hitting her face,
or too much noise hurts her head.

She told me of the medicine
she takes that makes her so sleepy.
She told me not to worry
and that she would never leave me.

I asked her why do they have them.

Mum said there is no real reason they get them.

Its just like the kids at school with coeliacs and food allergies she said.

No one can choose,

or see why they get them, it just happens.

Mum said we can just try our best to cope,

And trust that we will be strong together.

I asked how I can make her feel better,
and she said by lots of love and cuddles.
Mum said she is so sad because she can't
do as much for me but she still tries.

I know because she still goes to see me in my races at school, even though the wind hurts her face.

She still takes my brother and I to the movies,

even though you can see she can barely stay awake.

Mum told me that sometimes

she wont be able to get me from school.

But I should be careful

to only go with the people on our safe list.

Mummy said we are lucky to have family and friends to help.
So many other people don't have anyone to help support them or help them in anyway.

My mummy loves me and I love her.

I know now to just help in the house when I can.

Lay in bed and give her cuddles when she is sad.

Be quiet as I can when she has terrible headaches.

I try not to ask my mum to do things,
unless to me it is important to me.
But I don't have to
because my mum already knows.

My mum knows when I have
important things on at school.
She always shows up,
even if she needs to go to bed after.

She never forgets my birthday,

Or when I need to go

to swimming or dance.

She always encourages me to do the best I can.

Now I know why my mummy cries.

She loves me and my brother so much it hurts.

BUT.....

Together as a family I know

we can help mum feel a little better.

But that she will never be the same mum I first had.

Despite it all, my mum is a fighter

cause she fights for me and my brother she said.

She fights to stay strong and

do the best she can for us even if it hurts.

Lightning Source UK Ltd.
Milton Keynes UK
UKHW051613180920
370103UK00003B/35